twine

twine

poems by

John Diamond-Nigh

Kelsay Books

© 2018 John Diamond-Nigh. All rights reserved. This material may not be reproduced in any form, published, reprinted, recorded, performed, broadcast, without the express written consent of John Diamond Nigh. All such actions are strictly prohibited by law.

Cover layout by Shay Culligan

ISBN: 978-1-947465-96-1

Kelsay Books
Aldrich Press
www.kelsaybooks.com

For you who suggested the angles of this book

Acknowledgments

Thanks:

To Yoshi Kunimoto, brilliant composer who has created musical settings for many of my poems, and in doing so has enhanced and enlarged them.

To Gary Culbertson and Francisco Troconis of Contemporaneo, who so generously opened their gallery doors to me and permitted me the unusual opportunity to blend my poetry, furniture, sculpture and Yoshi's music into an Appalachian *Gesamtkunstwerk*.

To strangers and friends alike who have come to my readings. A reading is always a hypothesis which subsequent months of work must set out to prove true.

To Lynne, my wife, who is the first reader of what I write and whose nearly inerrant literary sensibilties remind me of those masterful gardeners in the parks of Paris who prune, discard and shape toward a better eventual leaf.

"Best Pens" and "For *Tomorrow*" appeared respectively in *The Paris Review* and *Agni*.

Contents

ontario

plain folk	15
poet	16
the wood of me	17
lands	18
palestine	19
thistles	20
priest of seeds	21
turning seed	22
bagging seed	23
a woods death	24
the great canadian street corner	25
florence	26
question	27
boyhood	28
tree house elegy	29
best pens	30
conversion boxing	31
strapping	32
parable	33
nearly died	34
pure	35
the bishop said	36

heresy

belief	39
prayer	40
frenzy well aligned	41
strange belief	42
the ark	43
heresy	44
end times	45

montaigne	46
dear ancestors 2	47
dear ancestors 3	48
below	49
saviours	50
please	51
fanatics	52
keith	53
the bricoleur's daughter	54

salvation

lid	57
the disappeared	58
mauve	59
varèse	60
chicken house	61
daffodils	62
ballroom chairs	63
rebirth	64
the worst storm i've seen	65
babylon	66
bernstein	67
halloween	68

ars amatoria

composition	71
jarvis barber	72
venice 2	73
cortázar	74
ray charles	75
williams	76
shadow	77
for tomorrow	78
savages	79
new pens	80
red	81

starry one	82
mg	83
saint-sulpice	84

paris

lindenwood	87
blackboard horses	89
talking	90
evening on the pont des arts	91
learning of calamity in the luxembourg gardens	92
basilica of saint-denis	93
venice 3	94
on our last day in paris	95
on my last day in paris 2	96
rue du montparnasse	97

About the Author

ontario

When I was baptized round may—
late may–the river was still cold
no one told me to hold my nose as I
was dunked backward the shrill water
riding the slim rails of my nostrils into
my lungs till I choked disgracefully thought
I'd die—could not catch my breath
a man nearby was mowing
his lawn like the man plowing
in breughel's fall of icarus
this time however he saw me
and laughed like hell
if I enumerate the shames
of religion its hardships
its doom-wishes its deaths
its few benevolences some were grave
others like its psalms its wisdoms
only ornate
like quantities of butter in old recipes
quaint riches we would never think
of using now but *plainness* stuck
perhaps not *stuck* it passed through other
increments—brancusi beckett
motherwell—until I found
it suiting my modernity
this well

plain folk

I say that I'm a poet only
rarely I don't even think
my family thinks I'm one—they don't—
a writer or a metaphoric
fantasist my father's grave
has grass upon it now that blends
with almost no distinction into
cemetery lawn his death
was forty years ago he never
thought I was a poet though
he hoped that I someday would be
a preacher that was poetry
enough for him—declamatory
eloquence my sisters never
ask me for a poem at
a birthday or a funeral
their children play their violins
instead to them a poet is
a recklessness that most of all
discredits family values it
is not a world where christians make
their mark—the arts—a grave's a pensive
thing a train runs by perhaps
the dead can hear the whistle in
their afterlives the rattle at
the junctions of the rails O go on
living in your death without
my poetry

poet

Pa I'd like a tractor ride
the snow so deep the air so still
I like the simple stubborn motor
barking at the stark bucolic
silence like an ecstasy
of grumpy saints I like your smell
your arms around me letting me
control the wheel its old corroded
plastic in my fingers we
could talk about eternity
the way men do in forests as
the trees are getting restless and
the snow drops down in fractured shawls
around us we may find a nest
or wrap the chain around a log
and pull it home your unshaved chin
against my neck like some old file
that works to smooth the grain of me–
a chair or some prospective shape
of being

the wood of me

I would ask him now looking
at this placid choir of furrows
why my father left toronto
after university strict
faith as he later might concede has both
its marvelous severities but
too its punitive
superstitions its blunt
political vengeances
plain faith—plainer even
than american shakers
dog house churches as a friend
put it with dogs inside (as I'd
come to understand) too plain
for cicero and sophocles
of course they drove you out the bald
anomaly these furrows running
straight from end to end is where
you fell your heart *attacked* again
this time the harshest *brother* of
them all I never called you *dad*
or built a doghouse not at least
with you I built it by myself
and painted it bright pink—my first
dissent from that solemnity
undeviating rigor of
a rural christianity
I'd ask with all those many years
of city education why
you couldn't have been a little bit
more tolerant or liked me just
a little

lands

One hand abstains another reaches
down and wipes the snow away
the long procession slowing at
the cemetery gates beneath
a black allée of cedars as
a bird itself like snow descends
and hovers on the coffin lid
just hovers there as if by some
enchantment I will think of you
as *border crosser* crossing at
the allenby to jericho
first citizen of any country
since the '67 war
to make that crossing. south and east
from london athens istanbul
damascus to amman and now
jerusalem *impossible*
each consulate insisted and
then sinai against all odds–
what odds were ever more to you
than slightly odd?—in lebanon
guerillas held you for a week
then let you go fed up I guess
with someone who was undercutting
them but was devoted to
the destitute so back you went
to work among the bombed and shrapneled
farmers making as you could
the disappointing sorts of peace
that war allows—then suddenly
the bird lifts off above the snow
your soul perhaps in its farewell
long phantom wings go swishing on
like lanterns of immaculate
aurora

palestine

Of all those tools the furniture
the implements of copper wood
or steel we had no trouble guessing
most of them a crescent spade
for airing grain a massive tapered
upright walnut column used
for making collars pliers made
of oak and almost four feet tall
still working smoothly—*crunch*—*for pulling
molars from a dinosaur*
that stumped us then one day a man
his hat almost as wide as a
sombrero black eyes glittering
remembered back to when there was
no running water then the first
electric light the farmer whipped
his boys bare-ass but christ the man
could think up tools and make them to
perfection once an implement
that cut and braided worn-out cloth
and made a rug his wife just turned
a wheel this odd-shaped paddle made
to beat his girls bare-ass his wife
as well and this—he picked the wooden
pliers up and stepped outside
and found a thistle growing by
the barn and pulled it up like I
pull candles from a birthday cake—
a marvel

thistles

At market thoughtful stern long-booted
men would ripple fingers through
the millet the alfalfa sniffing
fingertips or lightly twisting
seeds between the grindstones of
their crusty palms and stand quite still
adducing or perplexed as if
each small alfalfa seed contained
saskatchewan or uruguay
some mystery that took some time
divining while a sparrow might
fly down and take a crumb of millet
dropped between the gravel in
its beak and we would watch the seed's
ascension flowing east toward lake
ontario as if a tiny
moon was being launched across
a latitude of dreams

priest of seeds

Two tramps the usual
stick-figure bohemia
of the low townships knives angled
under a weak peach of light
in a tumble-down barn as remote
as bulawayo while I turn seed
airing the moist heat
they know me for a *holy roller*
passive not inclined to fight—
the hell I won't–they circle in
with gargled derogations jump
jump back jump in their knives out flat
like fangs I heave some millet seed
directly at their skinny eyes
a feint I take from basketball
then swing my shovel double like
an axe though wholly hampered in
the slush of seed I'm cut I'll soon
be dead another tramp goes down
two more appear and then a gun
goes off all freeze I hear my pa
I hear his low brick syllables
of consternation pa who never
held a gun in forty years
beside him henry pelham—hank—
a stoic rawhide pagan—hank
who sometimes took me fishing come
—his milking done—to scan some seed
hank wants to do the four of them
some 'good' and then he adds little
blood to that I never ever
thought of luck as *luck* again
I mended well
by christmas

turning seed

I loved the expert way my pa
would flick a length of twine a little
magic trick almost his way
of tying off a bag of seed
then adding it to all the other
bags of seed like warriors
asleep in some soft war of bird-winged
silence

bagging seed

evening I observe the partial
silhouette of someone who
is hanging in a murky huddled
copse of hawthorn just a bit
askew his feet are well above
the ground his arms outstretched he wasn't
naked like a crucifixion—
dressed but at a glance he wasn't
dressed too well a copper-colored
t-shirt still unusual
in winter where I'd come to cut
some branches for a dance and warm
my flute before our friends arrive
on horseback moon a mild blue wheel
above to see a man who if
he wasn't dead was hanging like
he would be

a woods death

I hear the old evangelist
he's standing on the sidewalk and
he's hollerin' for rain
a *vengeance* of rain a big
vengeance of rain—he made that up
on the spot—*a vengeance of rain* and pounds
the pestle of a fist into an open palm
didn't you hate
evangelistic services
some preacher from ohio or
missouri that great country who
would take the train to canada
my pew was just a plank a simple
board I always wondered if
they thought of us as pioneers
or worse as sticks I fidgeted
and listening if only in
an incidental way I formed
my pictures of america
the cherries and the rivers and
the kisses that I cherish
even now

the great canadian street corner

Look at all the scratches scorches
slashes that have been repaired
she points them out–a woman from
ohio who herself performed
the restoration—proud and young
or seems so—still to be the hand
employed on such a big important
painting this by rubens yes
you emulate the style of say
parmigianino yet you're using
paint that in the future can
be easily removed the paint
applied in tiny stitches so
on close examination you
can see it's not original
look close—she holds a magnifying
glass above the finger of
adonis *see the pattern?*—I
could almost be in canada
again that hour in april tiny
field birds tingling through me all
my furrows nearly straight

florence

Kim novak in the meadow—june
her hands go up and down like sable
fins inside the evening like
her body was conducting some
experimental orchestra
of recently cut hay she mouths
a single word we both agree
the word is great but has too many
bad associations like
a glass of wine left overnight
uncovered then we feed each other
bread and wine like priests on easter
morning with a little more
elation than might otherwise
have been the case–who knows we are
not priests I watch her eat a large
tomato eating only flesh
with tentative precision biting
carefully around the yellow
seeds a bird goes by she asks
a question

question

Here stood a house its absence shocks
the wood and glass and ornamental
columns only air—one tree
remains I'd say my bedroom was
approximately there and through
these branches late one night I saw
the old barn going up in flames
the tractor—there—a silhouette
a scherenschnitte tractor quite
incapable of moving *move*
you asshole you who pushed and pulled
the earth for 30 years now move
just 30 feet O jesus christ
just sit there let your tires burn
your gasoline explode all night
the fires spread around us barn
the first the big gymnasium
four yachts at the marina and
two giant quarry trucks within
a mile or two but that was once
a *once* it must be said diseased
with tragedy—who knew it then?
but too the lazy satieties
the deepening through life's impure
elysian exuberance
my grim cigars my windowsill
of snow and flowers—taken down
why dwell on those who did so now?
the arsons of insidious
combustion set and tended to
by christian men and women over
many years why make this more
than what it was? we turn away
perhaps we say goodbye we won't
return

boyhood

Broken floor and pleated leaf
of tin that was my roof so long
ago when I elected this tall tree
my high float—dwelling well above
—O many things—
the stony abolitions of
the township preachers harping on
and on about *work ethic* hardly
ethic hardly *harps* just brute
enslavement meant to obfuscate
desire what they denounced with upraised
arms as evils of the flesh
flesh—another word they got
all wrong—now forty years have passed
I climb my tree again I have
my old anthology beneath
my belt the brownings robert frost's
stone-syllabled old witches then
incantatory medieval
yeats with *innisfree* tattooed
across his rump and then a page–
one page that I have read so many
times the ink has worn away
–audacious sappho taking on
some dull bullheaded preacher praising
sins that we no longer
even have

tree house elegy

Once I'm sure there's no one else around
I climb bird-nimble toward my small house
held like a saucer on fingertips
in the middle branches of the tree
I wonder who's there
a light is on knotting a rope
to the uppermost branches I lower myself
over the roof skirting the eaves
until I reach the window ledge
clumped on my bed my cigarette case
my opera my best pens my first edition borges
my lindt chocolates my russian icon
already half-inserted in a bag
you pause for a moment listen then bend
again to your writing at my desk
using *my* best parker pen
I watch the slim tusk of your ponytail
your glossy leggings your slim intelligent legs
I watch you watch a moth
I remember reading that phillip glass
and richard serra would go to la coupole
just to watch giacometti eat his supper
paris on the brain my opera
takes place there too beginning
at baudelaire's *le club des hachichins*
where green jelly hashish was served
by a doctor on silver trays
baudelaire—maybe you're him
here to inspect my opera you gather my things
blow out the light and squeeze your bag
through the slender doorway down you go
I follow halfway down the tree
I jump but you have vanished

best pens

Pa what is death? I asked in some
far-off decrepit barn my pa
would pause and laugh another scoop
of timothy or millet sliding
down the shovel then he'd pause
and change the subject not exactly
change but tell a story which
perhaps would have some relevance
to what I asked my uncle paul
was famous through the townships for
his prowess boxed joe louis once
he even boxed the lord before
he got salvation—news to me–
he boxed the lord? he knocked our savior
down he cut his lip then paul
in turn went down and stayed there for
the count till jesus helped him up
and said now follow me

conversion boxing

My breakfast bowl of oatstuff shaped
in letters where by nudging them
in milk I'd spell *jerusalem*
or *rome* we never used those words
but still jerusalem was when
the bedroom door would shut a dresser
drawer disclose a narrow slab
of thrasher belt and when the act
of punishment was over I
misunderstanding your embrace
would stand erect not knowing how
to suffer knowing punishment
was hatred too then I would close
my bedroom door and find a book
beneath my mattress hands too hurt
too shamed to do much more than blindly
paw the pages till I came
to nicholas poussin a picture
painted in the countryside
just outside rome I didn't know
that much about poussin I simply
liked the hush of russet light
the still of time the broken temple
steps where gods had lived and passed
away

strapping

Come it's time that we made love
the stories all are over
the sun is drying out the veils
of timothy and clover

between your lips I tuck the stems
of every vow we've taken
and even as the evening falls
another evening wakens

I loved you as you came to me
I never made a play
disclose the tremors of your flesh
as promises you'll stay

I don't know why anxiety
is always part of love
the grass has woven to your hand
an inexplicable glove

parable

You're looking well your cheeks are pink
much better than a month ago
and I am still the fatalistic
worrier that can't be helped
we'll eat this bowl of cherries like
a daughter and a father would
with bluebirds in the hedgerow as
we talk and as you hum across
the limpid fields of grass beyond
the hedgerow–imperturbable
white farms where men go plowing after
breakfast women put up fruit
and vegetables for winter make
their flower gardens just as bright
as anything de kooning ever
painted—who would stain a day
like this with some tendentious new
disclosure

nearly died

Snow I'm sure had much to do
with who I am the list is much
too long for just one poem all
those obsolete simplicities
an uncle's farm a song by leonard
cohen where the trees resembled
colonnades in lebanon
then *paris* put that city in
italics beckett hemingway
when young the cars I drove were blunt
intrepid unadorned machines
that stopped in snowstorms would not go
another inch I pushed them to
the shoulder and I walked the blizzard
home the upright seat backs of
religion–fastened in as if
our life is just a flight of sinful
turbulence until my faith
that god may be became a purer
faith he's not noguchi smith
brancusi—going way way back
my father parked the car some empty
farmer's field across the field
a tent some horses tethered to
a temporary fence no other
soul around you felt the terror
glowing from that empty tent
and glowing from those horses

pure

Pa the bishop said this world
is getting worse my pa stands straight
though slowly back ain't quite the same
resilient steel it was when he
was conquerer of all rural
townships standing straight he does
a little stretch and sets his shovel
upright in the seed and laughs
it happens at this very moment
son I'd like some melon half
for you and half for me the juice
like sugar no the world ain't getting
worse for all my juvenile
penchant for contradiction pa
was right

the bishop said

heresy

make believe: you *make belief* a handiwork
      as someone makes religion or a chair
make believe: you are made to believe
      a condition of inclusion in
      a family tribe or mystical order
make believe: a game a tall tale
two rows of zinnias so straight
christ they might have been cut
on a table saw

belief

I haven't now for many years
at family do's when grace is said
shut eyes or bowed my head it's not
ingratitude but rather that
I wonder how few generations
back we'd have to go before
the faithful sitting here would burn
my schizophrenic sister in
a bonfire for possession by
unholy spirits really what
has changed in their theology
since the nicean council took
a vote on whether jesus was
divine? the prayer is over looking
right I see my sister looking
back at me and smiling

prayer

Thomas benton rendered corn
like light bulbs in a factory
I'd paint you just like that—don't move
the zinnias as impeccable
as furniture my illness as
complete as fifty chair legs all
identical just waiting on
their shelf to be one final time
touched up a little sanding then
the glue and the assembly we
have delicate machines we have
those methods that our literature
is asked to serve–the frenzies that
arise from such perfections we
align like eggs in cartons and
then grade them by their magnitudes
of silence

frenzy well aligned

Back then of course you'd be the one
they burned in front of what is now
the city hall a heretic
an infidel today you'd ride
your moto guzzi fleeing down
the freeway past salinas with
the image of a jaguar on
your jacket underwritten with
invective–*fuck all capital*
or *jesus saves with citibank*
all night toward the sierras down
that narrow line of unbelief
from now to zarathustra

strange belief

A boat is being built the world
can see the heavy keel is laid
perhaps it is a god this ship
who fills himself with what the preachers
call the lucky ones *elect*
of god the rain will come the giant
boat will lift and those who aren't
on board will perish tell me how
obtuse such gods must be they'd drown
some children playing hopscotch on
the sidewalk childish innocence
on par with theft or murder *change*
my god a thought that makes the dull
mirage of that great ocean liner
fade perhaps I choose to have
no god at all the days regain
their normalcy the autumn rain
comes down sometimes umbrellas hardly
help against the downpour water
pours into the basement then
the sun comes out two chickadees
are squabbling by
the puddle

the ark

You may be content being
one of the miscellaneous holy ones
hanging around the temple precincts
adoring a high priest who owes
his place to the totalitarian tribe
who overran our country a decade ago
then again what in this culture
of servitude and militant vanity
isn't false? the real guys
are the zealots in the hills
the artists in the orchards
the widows who once were
well-off but now must beg in
supplicant squalor always the first
with protest banners
when the state priests assemble
to amputate from scripture
anything displeasing to
the despots the moneybags
and murderers they serve—like them
I want to be a heretic

heresy

How often has religion turned
from being the original
dissension to becoming just
an ignorant recurrence of
the very world that first dissension
hated most a rose becomes
a narrow can of petals sealed
and labelled with doxologies
and dogmas expiration date
is *never* all mythology
is withered into literal
intransigent conviction yeah
a zealot in morocco is
a zealot in grand rapids call them
heretics except I like
the term too much—O mother says
the emperor of lilies didn't
I tell you in jerusalem
it all would come
to this

end times

I leave and when I've just come back
I leave again is that the way
montaigne thought?—a man who hated
cruelty one who lived through the
religious wars in france in which
the militant ferocity
of catholics and protestants
is hard to picture even now
along the beach a dog is going
crazy seeing dolphins leaping
up and splashes toward them in
the water owner laughs at what
a muddy mess he's making of
himself he'll have to put him in
the swimming pool back home and clean
him up–the owner throws a stick
the dog runs off in wide erratic
circles as the three of us
can't help but laugh—one day I'm *this*
he mutters then the next I'm *that*
the dog comes back he hurls the stick
again I think that auden says
that too somewhere we just pretend
we know what's going on this crazy
thing that's me—some days I'm even
that

montaigne

Dear ancestors I've told you this
before while at the gypsum mine
I met a mohawk who when still
a boy had known a man who had
my name a man well known across
six nations reservation helped
my parents out with money helped
a lot of folks he married uncle
dan he died quite suddenly
one night we heard his tractor hit
a fallen tree the big man touched
my shoulder smiled and turned
and swayed away

dear ancestors 2

Dear ancestors the furniture
of all your sober minds have I
implored the quiet mortises
of certainty the singing in
a dovetail joint the longing in
the grain of oak or rosewood shaped
in talismanic quietude
to be this chair that I am sitting
on

dear ancestors 3

Religion holds the hand of every
despot can you tell me why
I often for a class that I
was taking hung around the dump
in harrisburg a modern dump
the even himalayas of
detritus being shoved around
by robots once a perfect chair–
that got to me the furniture
imagined with such delicate
exactitude the joints combined
as tight as two hands holding leg
and seat that point of weakness still
locked tight like one entwining knot
of gracious flesh so visionary
so humane just lumped across
the heavy concrete sill and dropped
into the flames below

below

Wayne from bowen road my age
though taller strong as hell we'd venture
past the junk yard down the railway
through the woods as wayne picked out
the traces of the saviors all
we see at first are elderberries
black among the nettles then
we see the path their feet have worn
the canes their hands have stripped and there
the ashes of their campfires wayne
who knows the psalms by heart observes
the saviors come from many tribes
all speaking different languages
the way it was in babel if
you think of it this way the narrow
railway line now overgrown
but visible enough to see
its even elevation five
or six feet wide is like the ledge
of some great ziggurat uncoiled
and laid out flat a bum wayne says
is not a savior neither are
the convicts who escape along
the railway line we picked a night
then lost our nerve so never saw
their esoteric goings-on
those penny pharoahs once we found
a pair of shoes abandoned in
the underbrush their moody humid
splendor and their piety
gone out

saviours

Small fanatical distinctions
in how this or that was done
was it performed
in precise emulation of christ and who
really knew how christ did anything?
right hand or left or even how
you dunked a man immersing him
along the susquehanna this
small sect goes up to heaven this
whole planet goes to hell indulge me
once let the outlandishness
sink in? imagine faith as some
bewildered apprehensive grace
a brushing after meals around
the edges of the soul I think
god's sick of all our righteousness
could not care less what car we drive
she wanted life to be *just life*
the way she made it dubious
and sweet with downs and ups and downs
and ridden in the end like some
calm mustang into heaven

please

All the fanatics are having lunch
the waiter asks who slashed the painting
hanging in the met from top
to bottom then from side to side
a painting that some bishop in
montana called *the super bowl
of devils*–no that didn't help
but bring things down to earth of course
the painting was heretical
that's only to the good just think
of galileo in his time
voltaire the waiter knows that someone
eating his carpaccio
destroyed his favorite painting and
has gold and lilies certainly
salvation even women in
his pocket as reward

fanatics

The silo's ruined open end
at night when you looked up to watch
the stars would change their context–make
infinity seem something else
entirely just a ceiling forty
feet away cigars from keith
the bourbon too the hennessey
the masturbation all were myrrh
from keith enjoyed in that oblique
and starred seclusion dad a deacon
uncle was a bishop keith
magnanimous and gentle kid
as I was too would tear along
the boulevard a lazy fatal
snake of road his hand-me-down
blue ford would quake through every bend
the sycamores stepped closer once
he walked me through *agnosticism*
telling me he wasn't that
but worse he didn't care if god
was up in heaven he was here
in high school at important games
keith thought a little hennessey
would help I think it did I once
scored fifty points keith cheering in
the bleachers *hey—you fuckin' drunk*
you did it

keith

Just as the string quartet was tuning up
for an afternoon concert of vivaldi
a young girl shouldered a giant snowball
up the steps and through the doors
of grace presbyterian church
bare feet slipping as she inched the giant
globe along the narrow granite
aisle by intermission snow
was melting bits of junk revealed
inside the snow—a strange archaic
lamp some leaves the handle of
a rake a small clay pyramid
by concert's end I thought that lamp
particular significant
a husky broken splendor who
would bust a lamp that beautiful
in quite that way? no accident
but smashed by some bullheaded act
of rage its light run over and
extinguished but that hardly mattered
now each person sitting at
that concert saw the flash of light
inside the snow and then the rake
ascending

the bricoleur's daughter

salvation

Two carpenters a couple lots
away are taking time to build
a coffin all the tools are there
the unimpeded space the boss
has let them pick through cut-offs even
use new wood as needed it
is saturday the two young friends
are hard at work the one looks rough
and anxious mariachi music
plays below the dead he thinks
return to some primeval clan
somewhere among the stars he isn't
certain how our consciousness
persists is it a landscape or
an interval before we're born
to other lives a pencil in
his hand
he draws a spaceship on
the rippled lid

lid

They disappear the shilly-shallying
girl along the towpath or
the husband who went out for milk
a tall man climbs a stairway to
the sky eclipsed from view as wife
and daughter plead to come back down
by now we know the signs a vague
commotion in the attic something
not quite right an inkling or
a shadow on the wall now people
don't sit waiting off they run
as if by taking flight they will
elude the ineluctable
so we as well were running through
the woods you had your toothbrush I'd
forgotten mine it made you laugh
don't even think of going back
the rain let up it seemed that we
had outrun danger still you kept
on running hand still holding mine
long after it was gone

the disappeared

It's going to happen soon I'm going
to find another job without
this loss that just keeps buzzing in
my head a job beside a lake
where all around me flows such stony
grandeur O I'll have to get
the hang of certain tools you always
do I'll make new friends how gravely
cool will be the weather as
I'm doing what I'm doing painting
houses by the waterfront
or helping tourists up the slopes
for picnics city people who
are taken with the lupins and
the butterflies a small blonde girl
confides that she likes *mauve* she likes
the color *and* the word she spots
a butterfly with dots across
its wings of such recondite blue
she wonders if such butterflies
are spirits

mauve

The boy in the orange vest
whistles at america
across the street and up against
a window where he thought edgar
varèse once worked he gets around
the downtown streets he whistles like
a bird from some mosaic of
percussions–like magnetic tape
in some oblique apartment say
on clarkson street that's being cut
and spliced together then into
the chaos of existence being
played

varèse

Another house the pre-stressed concrete
walls are lowered into place
by lunchtime as I watch the final
panel bolted tight the massive
crane and tractor trailer backing
down the hill–too big to make
the curve above–the chickens start
to crow inside a house two lots
away an old victorian
that's caving in the windows gone
like boxers' splintered eyes a dozen
chickens live inside I hear
them singing every sunrise singing
mozart singing arvo pärt
I see them in the evening in
the trees now as the trucks depart
I hear their sweet archaic anguish
carried through the broken frames
alarm as old as that
of agamemnon

chicken house

Daffodils farewell these yellow
weeks their color almost makes
you cry goodbye I don't know why
I need to bring this up just now
but sally was a secretary
bored to tears she handed in
her resignation boss it seems
was caught off guard she took a chair
and watched a robin just beyond
the window so you're leaving I
have never had a daughter as
you likely know she lived a couple
hours and then she died not even
buried anywhere that was
the way things were back then who grasps
at twenty-one what ceremonies
mean I guess I still could have
a funeral but what would that
achieve? more sadness? hard to say
I often see my daughter in
the birds and you you'll write another
novel take these yellow pads
as many as you'd like–they say
our century will re-construct
the soul and bring it back into
the mainstream–like some eel that we
believed to be extinct a small
taboo that someone yesterday
declared that they heard singing in
the lilacs

daffodils

The gilded tawdry ballroom chairs
the furniture of illnesses
and broken-hearted weathers that
we think will last all night but never
do a woman lifts her skirt
not meaning to but does how weak
the chair appears to be she even
rocks a little pointing out
a tenon working loose inside
the mortise like a wooden tear
that weeps the weight of men who in
the darkness with their fingers shaking
touch the soft assent of breasts
the cigarettes and charred bouquets
of gin it makes you think of fields
of furniture in even rows
as men request another kiss
before they leave for war

ballroom chairs

I heard the term so often that
like all clichés it never meant
a thing and those who said that they
were so reborn were hardly ever
pictures of transcendence yes
some were though few of those became
religious there's a cave in crete
that starts out big but then gets very
narrow as you crawl toward one
last cavity that's deeper in
the rock until the stone in fact
constricts and you feel permanently
stuck of course you panic being
human try to concentrate
on writers who for many years
have meant the world to you not only
this but darker deeper worlds—
bachelard breton or freud—you think
of bluebirds in the cattails you
squeeze through

rebirth

You see the old philosophers
with cigarettes who seemed to smoke
each brand of man's unhappiness
right now I'm smoking greek a little
parthenon is on the pack
now picture it in darkness on
a stormy night a killer stormy
night I climbed the ramp to the
acropolis and scaled the metal
barrier and stood inside
the parthenon—the storm a monster
getting very bad the rain
and lightning at their worst—and then
abating—all alone in that
corroded dark perimeter
of colonnades the storm had passed
what oracles were singing?

the worst storm I've seen

Now is long ago and long
ago is even further in
the past what others tend to call
unconscious or the underworld
for me is just a place and time
a little vague but somewhere back
in paris—maybe couperin
zola they look like silhouettes
of water with their cigarettes
assembled in a small salon
and even more obscure to me
is who I am I sense a restless
sanctity then someone says
manet has fallen ill manet
is dying quite impossible
a silver woman stoops to say
adieu and sets—as though it were
an artifact from babylon–
a kiss beside the roses

babylon

A picture—leonard bernstein in
arcadia between composing
symphonies he's getting old
but still a beauty youthful hair
luxuriant—a god's though just
a photograph you almost see
it blowing in his bathing suit
he walks along the shoreline as
the water-colored jaguars in
the ocean walk beside him O
to live like this among the spit
and castles and the warbled songs
and silent universities
and lusts that flow through iron walls
the way we finish work of any
kind and wait impatiently
this naked to the sun to start
again

bernstein

Waiting for snow one halloween
war and snow
both predicted to start around eight
the hallway is full of the lunatic bunch
from my greek tragedy class I look—
iphigenia agamemnon
oedipus a quick count of heads
tells me everybody's here
though who is who is hard to say
knock knock—my turn to get the door
cold I watch the dappled rays
of flashlights just before me stands
a small girl as an astronaut
I ask her what the earth looks like
from outer space I know of course
from pictures how serene and blue
and silent ask what candy she
prefers she picks a mars bar *mars*
appropriate I laugh I want
to kneel into the silence of
the tender snow I want to light
all black sardonic oils in me
in homage to each flake of life's
eternity instead I turn
to close the door her mother tells me
cleveland's just been bombed the snow
diaphanous and scanty first
is coming in a downpour now
beginning like the war a little
early

halloween

ars amatoria

A small bouquet of daffodils
a lady swings the door the room
is dark with fumed mahogany
and brass a late brancusi on
a pedestal picassos on
the wall a servant enters with
a silver tray upon the tray
hashish like baudelaire a silver
bowl with melted chocolate she's
invited to remove her skirt
and lay across his lap her buttocks
naked now the chocolate that
his mother sent from istanbul
is bitter as she sucks his fingers
sedulously clean then asks
if mama knows just how *outré*
her chocolate is then laughs he takes
his felt-tipped pen in hand and starts
to write across her skin a land
of pools and fissures rain and clouds
and grass and streams of reeds that's how
at ten each night he makes each poem
up there is no second draft
no crossing out all errors are
the heresy the burnt *éclat*
of love

composition

I'm building this dark chair to be
an idol when the parts are all
assembled you and all the world
will know how much I love you these
smooth legs the tenons clamped into
the mortises as if a man
who knew you needs reminding how
your hips and forehead moved like flights
of birds the men in jarvis barber
stood to see you walking by
the stupid shit they said just call
that poetry the ways the wind
would curl your skirt like grass your high-
heeled shoes the way they sang against
the sidewalk in their supple chains
of rain

jarvis barber

If it's said I killed myself
in venice they might say as well
that you were drinking wine in the
palazzo that was just next door
to leonardo mortuary
saw the gondola emerge
go gliding off into the mist
the coffin draped with lilies for
cremation out somewhere in the
lagoon a golden eagle on
the coffin lid you turned and gave
the downpour of your adventitious
lust to one–a gentleman
from cambridge–looking out at the
canal you had more wine you told
your stories on the tintoretto
bed and then you reached across
the dark vermilion water and
turned off the moon

venice 2

We do agree—a corridor
though can't concur on wing or floor
I say you had your retinue
of students like a mother has
her rope of chicks around your perfect
head a smoky ghost was hard
at play as all eternal things
I came to understand were always
making love to your percipient
gaze your movie actress eyes
effulgent lips your evening lengths
of thighs I saw the authors that
you loved not as the boisterous
bohemians they were but as
immaculate aristocrats
old lovers now who having shaken
off impulsive ardors were
though wholly immaterial
encasing you with whispering
precision as you walked I saw—
I couldn't say for sure garcía
lorca or cortázar then
it vanished as you quivered through
your loveliness like music
from a horn

cortázar

How many years how many lives
just waiting at the corner for
a glimpse a shadow waiting in
the solemn sloppy drench of all
these footsteps going up and down
3rd avenue there are in certain
symphonies a single note
you learn with some amusement to
expect if not amusement as
a cue to passion knowing in
that single note a naked body
circulates a vine of warm
complexity a vase of perils
standing in the crowd I heard
your footstep first by then we both
were well into our thirties getting
old or getting young into
the radiance of how your slender
heel upon the sidewalk made
the rain sound just a little like
ray charles

ray charles

I sorted through the letters william
carlos williams sent to friends
like ezra pound and even t.s.
eliot and pound's replies
from rappalo were full of lines
if not erased run over with
a purging playful overwriting
text the highest floor of the
humanities department where
I spread the letters out like sheets
of snowdrops not facsimiles–
originals that summer there
were picnics at professors' homes
the talk went on past derrida
foucault until montaigne in
the swimming pool then drinks that we
invented just so we could name
them basquiat or dunham you
the only woman there who never
swore and when you touched me I
believed at once so much like sudden
converts to religion full
of gratitude and rigor there
would never be a tyrant in
america and books would ring
the world and teach the heartache of
democracy a chickadee
had made you laugh so hard I had
to prop you up you took my arm
and kissed me

williams

Our small cat licks her shadow on
the wall each sunny day she sits
as we are drinking coffee and
she licks her silhouette my wife
despairs and then she laughs we both
can't help but laugh and then I think
a cat's imagination how
should I presume to know what's up
with that or just what symbol of
uncertainty or joy is being
indicated—scripture of
a sort or even gratitude
for all that's evanescent

shadow

Once it seemed so easy to go on
our language second nature *hammer stair*
foundation joist or *header* then one day
your word for *rafter* changed a bit off key
your word for *sash* was *such* at first
we laughed
my *mortar* sounded close to your *tomorrow*
then *tomorrow* changed into a kind
of warble unlike any sound
I knew by then you might as well
have been a bird–your language wasn't
human anymore perhaps
you didn't even have a word
for *yesterday* for *now* or for
tomorrow then at coffee break
my *sugar* made you cross you threw
your hammer in the weeds it caught
my foot what else was there to do?
we gathered up our tools a final
time shook hands and went in two
directions almost enemies
already

for tomorrow

If poetry's one thing or two
a light bulb or a little glass
of daffodils with fingertips
that touch the hand of god why can't
those daffodils be just a pack
of lies as well with fingertips
that reach the same transcendence—why?
a savage at the bar picks up
the little vase and hurls the flowers
down and then he crushes them
beneath his metal boots he swigs
a cataract of beer and asks
how anyone can really tell
the difference and if the lies
look good to him he'll just keep bidding
up the lies until they have
the look of truth his broken urns
of fists contain the sermons that
he listens to on sunday all
the hymns and greed and pickup trucks
and paranoia all that pseudo
weather shit come on you silky
bastards who would dare I'll *smash
your face into gazpacho*—as
a woman who has seen too much
of rural fallibility
sweeps up the shattered daffodils
with fingers that are sobbing

savages

My baby gave me yesterday
a fountain pen for christmas made
in italy the finest pen
I've ever had the ink a gleaming
black and green and then I lick
my thumb and lift another sheet
of paper made in italy
as well I pause my wife suggests
I write a word as beautiful
as all of these together I
write *cabbage*

new pens

We signed our declaration on
the snowflakes of your skin and then
I kissed the cold enchanting soot
of wine around your nipples ate
a little plate of bussolà
then dipped my head between your legs
translating all the sweet decay
of passion every stem of murmur
back to its majestic red
again

red

Repair the moon it's waning too
unevenly it's not quite right
and so you take your box of tools
your arcane lunar implements
and start to climb indeed you find
a rivet in the light that's working
loose so vast the moon up close
your paltry box of tools might seem
inadequate and yet repairs
are made the light regains its former
luster and its perfect sickle
edge of smoothness now you'd like
a beer the climb exhausted you
the only thing you didn't bring
along to this preposterous
domain of light—more fucking fool
you get it seems with every passing
day sometimes with every passing
hour but then you get back home
you're very very thirsty now
the moon at that proximity
can dry you out so open the
refrigerator sitting on
the second shelf your sandwich and
a beer the simple lunch your wife
prepares before she goes to work
beside your lunch a card that calls
you *starry one* or *honey*

starry one

Turning round the corner by
san marco classic sports cars find
a straightaway ahead and gun
their engines roaring farther south
eventually to rome two hundred
cars or more the drivers wave
and laugh their scarves like amaryllis
blossoms back inside the heavy
monastery walls I still
can hear the motors passing by
I fall into a painting of
a crucifixion—woman on
a cross and from a cauldron like
a stick an upright snake its head
so like a polished glans of bluish
jade—a painting long caught up
in controversy such that it's
a wonder that it's even placed
on view today *promiscuous*
emergencies as leonard cohen
put it that arise and then
against all odds remain however
slashed and burned and then repaired
this mute illicit dolphin this
volcano that emerged from such
profundities we only can
pretend to understand outside
more cars go by how many cars
can any rally have it's like
a river

mg

My self-commission years ago
was linger take some candles—well
I took a lot of candles—from
a chapel to the right I needed
candles for a sculpture and
I paid what the donation box
suggested I had tried to find
a priest I sewed a long cloth bag
to smuggle six or seven candles
out each evening no it wasn't
theft I paid but who outside
would know? O france! a sculpture that
would bear I hoped some flavor of
my sacrilege but mostly what
I wanted was the *holiness*
the million ardent martyrdoms
that flutter through the darkness of
your tyrannies in short I wanted
all your terror paris in
my piece

saint-sulpice

paris

Out of the paris metro fifteen
sixteen priests climb up the stairs
their costumes pleated like origami
reptiles even the cut of their beards
arresting—shaped to esoteric
effect each man grand and tall
black lines hedge their difficult eyes
gnostic if I had to guess
though that's just me the bit I know
of gnosticism colored by
the cathars jung and legacies
of romance all those places where
old heresies still go to hide
in paris or in williamsburg
I'm sure I'm wrong these grand tall men
suspend your gaze they really do
ignoring us their dark eyes set
ahead of them they climb the stairs
in two straight lines—you have to think
of madeline—they're carrying
a slender box too long to be
a coffin on their shoulders antique
lindenwood the symbols carved
with sensual exactitude
the loops and buds and crosses—was
it just the light or was there some
idealism hurt and charred
and leaking from that lindenwood
toward sense

lindenwood

God may point and ask you
to come to the board and draw a horse
a horse can I remember what
a horse looks like?
the best I get—a stumpy provisional
silhouette an inept weathervane—but have
I told you in
the interest of your research how
men who sweep the streets employ
the same twig brooms that sweepers used
on rue vavin how gardens smell
like pancakes in the evening how
it never is exactly day
or night? but back to the shape of horses
how at the brink of memory
each effort at imitation takes
you further from the truth and so
in spite of knowing better what
you get is a horse that's square its tail
in the air like a pomeranian's
—o plato's ideal horse my dear—
and only a last impulsive flash
of recollection lets you see
how far you are from the truth although
you think you could be accurate
if you had to be if the final exam
of existence let's say was to *draw a horse*
but nostalgia itself begins to fade
and that's the worst nostalgia of all
leaving only delicate fragments
of all those shapes that drenched our lives
the bric-à-brac of a blurred mirage
that desperately reinvents itself
until you find there's nothing left

return to childhood you ask return
to earth I hardly know enough
to know how gladly
I would

blackboard horses

No that wasn't talking that
was talking as the morning rolled
the sidewalks out and set the trees
up straight and sang a car horn forth
in shrill stravinsky dissonance
while anne would speak for jean genet
émile for sartre andrew for
the bishop of amiens and you
agnostic of a thousand broken
coffee cups and cigarettes
between those fingers gracq compared
to subtle punctuation–*wrong*
for you is almost always right
the heresies of paris as
you like to say have taught the world
what metaphorical existence
is beyond the ways the church
and state and money say
the big world works

talking

Man from the new yorker–right?
here to tell your american readers
where on the rue du bac you buy
your oysters and wine how the old cafés
are all in the hands of syndicates now
perhaps a piece about supper with me
holed up here in the balthazar
with a cat half pickled in armagnac
it's true I did know beckett what
would you like me to say our last good chat
was out near rochefoucauld I think
some anodyne hotel does that
surprise you please I need a hand
we'll take a walk you'll help me down
the stairs how often anymore
do I get to see a sunset from
the pont des arts? dear boy those years
are fable now—genet camus–
which makes my anonymity
both worse and better hold your arm
just so my *archer's eye* now tell me
how in the world did you get your hands
on that? but yes you're quite correct
it happened here the story based
on abélard and héloïse
entirely forgotten as far as I know
I had forgotten it tell your readers
that–beside the armagnac–
how things that once were all the rage
a case in point my *archer's eye*
fall out of favor still I don't
complain I had my moment in–
O god how wild and high the moon–
primes pass

evening on the pont des arts

April morning standing in
the luxembourg a woman in
her metal chair as children pass
like christmas pageant marys on
their donkeys under expertly
espaliered trees the branches pruned
like angel wings we just were wiping
clean two chairs beneath a tree
when down the path two students ran
quite out of breath to tell us tod
was gone he'd run away to rome
enticed by some australian man
he'd met online his suitcase packed
he'd dropped some hints but no one thought
he'd do it—now this student in
our custody was somewhere down
a rabbit hole to rome O christ
O christ O christ more calls to make
the dean the parents blowing up
a pentecost of lies across
the internet our stories do–
our stories run away with us–
one story to another let's
go fishing have a picnic let's
scare all the pigeons in the park
in one great ruffling scarf and while
we're at it scare some people too
I look again—he's there his suitcase
tilting from his hand it seems
a change of heart—a woman settles
down to read her proust beneath
the chestnuts and another donkey
wobbles by *O paradise*
O city

learning of calamity in the luxembourg gardens

Shutter timed at seven seconds
hoping that she doesn't move
a perfect shot a woman at
the altar with her grocery bags
a crumpled shawl across her head
that line—I don't agree with it
that line between we mortals and
divinity what preachers called
the common rail the furniture
of penitence a line you came
to kneel at but a line you never
crossed the camera clicks another
cluck in the cathedral as
she rises to her feet and takes
a grocery bag in hand adjusts
her worn-out scarf then kneels again
and turns to watch a pigeon maybe
two—the holy ghost I take it–
edging in and pecking at
her groceries

basilica of saint-denis

I tell the gondolier I'll be late for class
confident my trousers pressed knowing
when it comes time to speak
I'll think of something marc chagall's
gnostic cows or giacometti's
little clouds we dock at the private
marble wharf on the dot of ten
my students waiting on the white steps
dressed in their knowledges of matta
pink sea blinking on their faces
in the spit-and-polish rooms I'll ask
them to choose a painting they hate
can make no sense of and tell us why
when it's my turn to speak
I'll improvise something on the silver
cauliflower I saw in the window
at buccellati's about how sacred
imitation is how we continually
make up new ornate similes
for old forms of pain
something perhaps about vegetables
in art or the place of fruit in human passions
thinking of you already in paris
stopping to buy some cherries for breakfast
then after that monique's to shower
toweling the fall of your sunburned breasts
fingering your nipples till
I taste them on my distant tongue

venice 3

On our last day in paris you got
your hair cut in a new salon
the stylist's immense paws
tossing your fresh hair like hay
I stopped at taschen
flipping through books
on the *demi-monde* vague
esoteric orgies in some oblique
époque we ate late lunch near danton's
statue stopped for chocolate
enough for all on the overnight train
to italy a fight broke out
not twenty feet from st eustache
between two pimps the sirens bristled
closer please young man get up
get up eustache cathedral where
last night the o-so-gallic jean
guillou played bach and liszt played
fucking thunder on the van den heuvel
organ jesus christ the old
church wobbled as we left we laughed
recalling how an organist
in antwerp told us jean guillou
was satan—others said the same
of liszt we kissed
our concierge good-bye just as
the rain began we asked our cab
to stop on rue d'assas and let us
kiss the sidewalk hands uplifted—
bishops of no other faith
than this persistent fragrant paris
rain—*young man*
get up

on our last day in paris

On my last day in paris
I got lost
stopping by a garden of
anarchic irises behind
an iron paling looking like demonstrators
skirted by the cops and held for
banging their flagrant petals on car roofs
just a block or two from giacometti's
studio in a part of town
called plaisance ironically pleasantness
where poor iron-mongers surrealists street-pavers
once lived beyond the montparnasse station
I was so lost—so turned around
I wondered if this city's tenebrous arms
were trapping me in some warm maze
of baking bread embroiderers
at work on the sidewalk children playing
hopscotch—little gentlemen
and ladies—dogs and diffident
old codgers in cafés the sirens
tolling soft recondite notes
against the sidewalk knowing yes
we're meeting on the pont des arts
our supper reservation made
for eight our final evening in
the city yet I hesitate
to find myself again by simply
asking some pedestrian
to point me toward *alésia*
the station where cartier-bresson
one rainy day snapped giacometti
coat above his head like one
hunched wing

on my last day in paris 2

each one of us must die as soon
as any god imagines us
who knows if that is true—it was
an aphorism written on
a napkin in a small café
on rue du montparnasse that day
a man was on the terrace making
tranquil annotations in
a paperback retired civil
servant by the look of him
his suit a little worn the pen
by contrast quite an opulent
pearlescent beauty edging close
I watched him fill the margins of
his bertrand russell paperback
with grocery lists and musings on
existence

rue du montparnasse

About the Author

John Diamond-Nigh is an artist, furniture- and award-winning interior designer, as well as an art and literature professor. For most of his career he and his wife spent a semester each year teaching in Paris or Florence, living, when in Paris, in Montparnasse among old, tumultuous spirits. For many years he co-authored a column called The Better World for the Pennsylvania magazine, Mountain Home. He has published two books, a book of poetry from York Press, and, more recently, a book of short fiction called Sacred Sins from Black Scat Books. He now lives in Asheville, North Carolina, where, with his wife, he built a home for his wife and himself in a secluded valley called Chicken Hill–aptly named since wild chickens still live in the trees and a rooster named Charlemagne never lets him sleep past six in the morning.

www.ingramcontent.com/pod-product-compliance
Lightning Source LLC
Chambersburg PA
CBHW031000090426
42737CB00007B/614